William Blake, 1757-1827

Blake's

Pencil Drawings

SECOND SERIES

EDITED BY GEOFFREY KEYNES
FOR THE NONESUCH PRESS
1956

Printed and made in Holland

THE LIST OF CONTENTS

iii

BLAKE'S PENCIL DRAWINGS
SECOND SERIES

It is nearly thirty years ago that the Nonesuch Press published a volume of *Blake's Pencil Drawings*, eighty-two pages of drawings being reproduced. The editor's Preface briefly surveyed Blake's achievement as a designer, and, in glancing at the sources from which the pencil drawings had been drawn, it was suggested that further volumes of the same kind might be compiled, since so many other drawings were known to exist; there was also the likelihood that other drawings previously unknown might come to light. In fact, not many new drawings have been found during this long interval. Nevertheless there is more than enough material to furnish a further volume, though the rise in costs of book production has dictated a reduction in the number of subjects chosen from eighty-two to fifty-six. As before, these range from Blake's earliest to his latest work, though again a preponderance has to be given to the later drawings, largely owing, it may be supposed, to the activity of his friend John Linnell in preserving the products of his pencil as well as his more finished pictures.

Designs which were not taken beyond the initial stage of a pencil drawing are often difficult to place in their proper chronological sequence, so that the ordering of the list is to some extent arbitrary. There can be no doubt, however, that the drawing of "The Penance of Jane Shore", made for the water colour drawing now in the Tate Gallery, is the earliest to which an approximately correct date can be assigned. Blake included the picture in his exhibition of 1809, remarking in *A Descriptive Catalogue* that it had been "done above Thirty Years ago", so that 1778 is its probable year. He was then a youth of twenty-one trying his hand at the fashionable practice of "historical" composition.

No date has been assigned for the next two designs for illustrations to *Macbeth*. The water colour drawings for Shakespeare's Plays recently acquired for the British Museum were done in 1806, but Blake had always studied Shakespeare closely and there can be little doubt that he began making designs for the plays long before this. The drawing of "Macbeth and the Ghost of Banquo", with its rather stiff lines, has the appearance of being an early composition; "Lady Macbeth and Duncan" is in a different style and is probably later, but it seemed sensible to place these two together.

Drawings for the great series of colour prints produced in 1795 were well represented in the former volume, but it was remarked that a drawing of great beauty for "Newton" was not then available. This omission is now remedied and the drawing will be seen to have much of the nobility of the finished composition, though it does not indicate the fact, noticed by Miss Kathleen Raine in the colour print, that Newton is sitting at the bottom of the sea, water being the symbol of materialist thought.

The Note Book (Rossetti MS) provided a number of sketches for the earlier Illuminated Books, but this source was used extensively in 1927; apart from a sheet of figure studies, the only drawing for these books now included is one for the frontispiece of *Ahania*, shewing Urizen, the god of Reason, crushing Ahania, his imaginative counterpart. An amusing drawing of "The Infant Hercules throttling the Serpents" also belongs, it is surmised, to this period, being sketched on the back of a fragment of poetry, "A Fairy leapt upon my knee", assigned to c. 1793.

Blake made a great number of illustrations for the Bible, both Old and New Testament, yet it is remarkable how few pencil drawings for these are known to have survived. Biblical subjects were represented in the first collection chiefly by designs for poems on biblical themes by Milton and for Blake's own Vision of the Book of Job. One New Testament drawing is included here, done for a tempera painting now in the United States of America, representing "The Virgin Mary hushing the young Baptist". Here Blake seems to symbolize the mother-child relation by the massive and dominating figure of the Virgin protecting her infant from the interference threatened by the eager child St John with his butterfly.

For the period of Blake's sojourn at Felpham there is a sketch of his faithful Kate, done about 1803. Her homely appearance and downcast eyes, intent upon some domestic task, suggest the relationship that always existed between the visionary artist and his modest companion.

It was probably in 1807 that Blake was making his designs for *Paradise Lost*. In the first volume of drawings only two studies for these were included, and it must now be confessed that one of them is not by Blake. It has been pointed out that a series of illustrations for *Paradise Lost* were made by a less well-known artist, Edward Francis Burney (1760-1848), and published in an edition of the poem in 1799. There are remarkable resemblances between these and Blake's designs and it is clear that Blake had not only seen them, but also allowed himself to borrow ideas from them. The drawing of "Adam and Eve sleeping" (no. 35 in *The Pencil Drawings*, 1927) is now seen to be by Burney and not by Blake, though the confusion is perhaps excusable. In the present volume four drawings for *Paradise Lost* are reproduced, two on plate 13 being sketches for Adam and Eve kissing in their bower, and it need not be feared that these were done by Burney. Another Miltonic drawing of "The Descent of Peace" for the *Ode on the Nativity* is also included, under the date c. 1809, when Blake was making his series of water colour drawings for this poem.

Work done in the year 1808 is represented by three drawings related to the designs for Blair's *Grave*, but all of these are quite different from the published engravings. A sketch for the tempera painting of Gray's "Bard" presumably belongs to 1809, the date of the tempera painting of this subject, and a careful drawing of "The Last Judgment", strengthened by having been inked over, is to be assigned to the year 1810, when Blake wrote his description of his "Stupendous Vision", as he called it. "I have represented it as I saw it", he added; "to different people it appears differently as everything else does; for tho' on Earth things seem permanent, they are less permanent than a Shadow, as we all know too well".

It was probably in 1815 that Blake attended the class room at the Royal Academy in order to make a drawing of the Laocoön group for an engraving in an encyclopaedia. This drawing is not of any special interest in itself, but is reproduced here for comparison with the next drawing—Blake's own version of the theme, which he has invested with all the power of which his pencil was capable. This fine drawing was exhibited at the Burlington Fine Arts club exhibition in 1876, but has remained almost unknown since that time. It is so large that it has had to be considerably reduced for reproduction, though, even so, much of its splendour still remains. The priest of the antique group now represents Blake's Jehovah, the Creator, in travail with his two sons, Satan and Adam. A finished picture of this subject would have been an exciting work, but the drawing is not known to have been taken any further.

Jerusalem, the last of the Illuminated Books, was in preparation from 1804 to 1820, so that the subjects belonging to it cannot usually be even approximately placed. Two drawings for this are included with several others possibly related, though not identified in its pages. One of these, "The Bowman", was in the collection of the late Graham Robertson, but had not previously been recorded or identified as Blake's work, although both idea and draughtmanship are characteristic.

In the years 1819 and 1820 Blake was amusing his friends Varley and Linnell with his series of Visionary Heads, as they have come to be called, or, in other words, imaginary portraits of persons who were supposed to appear to him in order to be drawn. Several of these were reproduced in 1927, and some more are added here, including a remarkable and previously unknown head called "The Spirit of Voltaire" and an attractive conversation piece of "Joseph and Mary and the Room they were seen in" —a touching suggestion of an adolescent love affair. An amusing profile of Gray on the same sheet as a drawing of Friar Bacon suggests that Blake sometimes depended for his "vision" on a portrait of the subject seen elsewhere. A drawing of "Old Parr when young", with its magnificent physique, is almost worthy to be called a portrait of one of Blake's Ancient Britons, though in fact it was incorporated in one of the drawings for the Divine Comedy.

Blake's pencil studies for most of his twenty-one woodcuts in Thornton's *Virgil*, 1821, were reproduced in 1927. He made no more woodcuts, though he made a drawing of the Prophet Isaiah on a woodblock, which was never engraved; a study for this is given here. Belonging to the same year, 1821, is a sketch for the elaborate symbolical painting called "The Circle of the Life of Man", discovered in 1947 at Arlington Court in Devon. The drawing had been misinterpreted until the finished work was found, since it omitted many important features of the more complete composition. It can now be properly related to its subject.

The last six years of Blake's life were largely devoted to his designs for *The Book of Job* and Dante's *Divine Comedy*, so that the latest pencil drawings are inevitably chiefly of these subjects. He did, however, start making a series of designs to illustrate *The Book of Enoch*, first translated into English from an Ethiopic manuscript in 1821. The first of these five drawings was reproduced in 1927, but has been repeated here in order that the whole number of these slight, though beautiful, drawings could be included.

Lastly Blake's portrait drawing of John Linnell, dated 1825, is inserted after those done for *The Book of Job* and before those for Dante, as a reminder that he was both the instigator of Blake's greatest inventions and the generous benefactor who made it possible for him to live his last years in freedom from anxiety and want.

The decision to include another early drawing was made too late to put it in its proper place in the sequence and it was accordingly substituted for a less interesting subject among the "Visionary Heads". This fine drawing is usually known as "God creating the Universe", though, as will be seen from the accompanying text, it may really represent the earth-bound rational man rather than God and thus be a precursor of the drawing of "Newton".

The reproduction of each drawing is accompanied by a brief commentary, with a statement of the size of the original sheet and its present location. Grateful acknowledgement is hereby made to the institutions and private owners who have kindly provided prints with permission to use them in this volume.

GEOFFREY KEYNES

I

THE PENANCE OF JANE SHORE

THE PENANCE OF JANE SHORE

ABOUT 1788

A sketch for the water colour drawing now in the Tate Gallery done about the year 1778. This pencil drawing is therefore the earliest to which an approximately correct date can be assigned. The finished picture shews the heads of many more soldiers behind the central figures than the drawing, but the resemblance of the two is otherwise close.

Jane Shore was the mistress of Edward IV and was known as a lady of great charm and discretion; yet, after the King's death, Richard III ordered the Bishop of London to make her walk in St Paul's Church in open penance, a taper in her hand and clad only in her kirtle. Blake wrote of the painting in *A Descriptive Catalogue*, 1809, p. 65; "This Drawing was done above Thirty Years ago, and proves to the author... that the productions of our youth and of our maturer age are equal in all essentials".

The pencil sketch belonged formerly to Mrs Alexander Gilchrist and later to Dr Greville Macdonald.

12 $^{1}/_{2}$ × 19 IN.   SIR GEOFFREY KEYNES

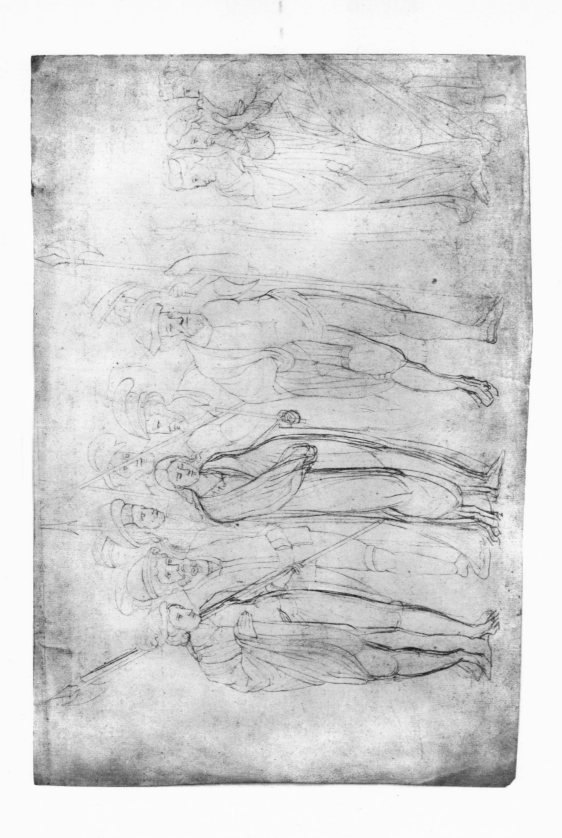

2

LADY MACBETH AND DUNCAN

LADY MACBETH AND DUNCAN

A rapid sketch of Lady Macbeth, with a taper in her left hand and a dagger in her right, hesitating at the door of Duncan's chamber. The head and shoulders of the sleeping form of the King is seen on the right. Inscribed on the left, sideways: "Had He not resembled my Father I had done it. Macbeth".

Given to the British Museum by John Defett Francis in 1874.

$6^{1}/_{4} \times 7^{1}/_{2}$ IN.   BRITISH MUSEUM

Had he not resembled my
father I had done it.

Macbeth

3

MACBETH AND THE GHOST OF BANQUO

MACBETH AND THE GHOST OF
BANQUO

A large and rough pencil drawing of a subject which does not appear to have been taken any further. Macbeth's terror and the impassivity of the other guests are well contrasted.

From the collection of Richard Johnson, sold in 1912.

14 $^{1}/_{2}$ × 20 IN.   SIR GEOFFREY KEYNES

4
FIGURE STUDIES

FIGURE STUDIES

Rough sketches of a variety of nude figures for unidentified subjects.

Given to the British Museum by John Defett Francis in 1874.

$6\,^{1}/_{4} \times 7\,^{7}/_{8}$ IN.   BRITISH MUSEUM

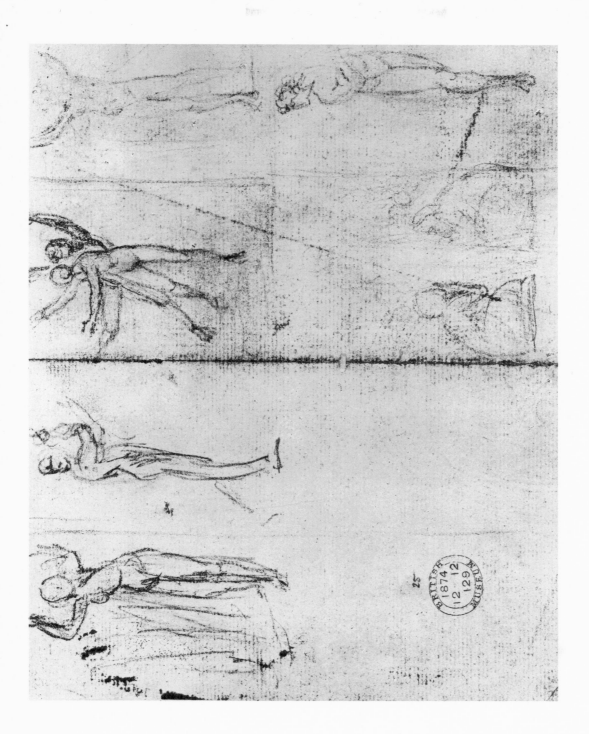

5
THE INFANT HERCULES THROTTLING THE SERPENTS

THE INFANT HERCULES
THROTTLING THE SERPENTS

ABOUT 1793

This subject is sketched on the back of a sheet carrying a poetical fragment beginning: "A fairy leapt upon my knee", c. 1793 (*Poetry and Prose*, ed. Keynes, 1939, p. 104). It was seen by A. C. Swinburne, who described it in his *Critical Essay*, 1868, p. 143 n., as: "a pencilled sketch of Hercules throttling the serpents, whose twisted limbs make a sort of spiral cradle around and above the child's triumphant figure: an attendant naked, falls back in terror with sharp recoil of drawn-up limbs; Alcmena and Amphitryon watch the struggle in silence, he grasping her hand".

Formerly in the collection of D. G. Rossetti.

$7^{1}/_{4} \times 5^{3}/_{4}$ IN.

ROSENWALD COLLECTION, NATIONAL GALLERY
OF ART, WASHINGTON, D.C.

6

JOSEPH OF ARIMATHEA PREACHING TO

THE INHABITANTS OF BRITAIN

JOSEPH OF ARIMATHEA PREACHING
TO THE INHABITANTS
OF BRITAIN

ABOUT 1794

Joseph of Arimathea, according to legend the first man to preach the Gospel of Christ in Britain at Glastonbury, stands on the right with his arm outstretched, preaching to a group of men and women. The drawing is one of three pencil sketches for the brilliantly coloured monotype of 1794 included in *The Small Book of Designs*, now in the British Museum, Department of Prints and Drawings. Two of the three studies are in the A. S. W. Rosenbach collection, the third is in the Rosenwald collection, National Gallery, Washington, D.C. A second impression of the monotype is also in the Rosenwald collection.

The provenance is unknown.

$13\,^1/_2 \times 19\,^5/_{16}$ IN.

PHILIP H. AND A. S. W. ROSENBACH FOUNDATION,
PHILADELPHIA, PA.

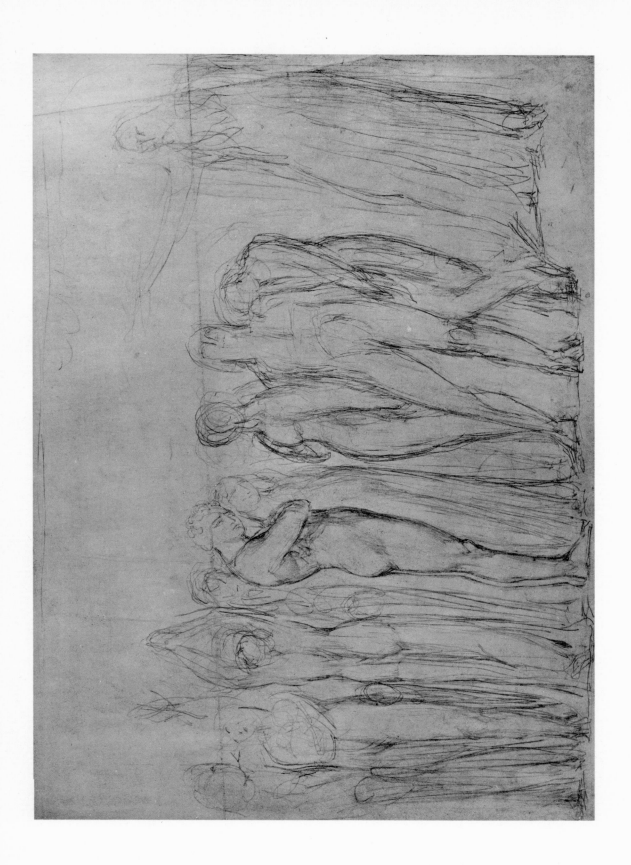

7

URIZEN AND AHANIA

URIZEN AND AHANIA

1795

A study for the frontispiece of *The Book of Ahania*, 1795. The massive figure of Urizen is seated with bowed head. Between his legs kneels Ahania, his Emanation, in an attitude of supplication. Urizen's huge hands appear to be gripping Ahania's head by her hair.

Given to the British Museum by John Defett Francis in 1874.

6 $^1/_4$ × 5 $^1/_8$ IN.   BRITISH MUSEUM

8

SIR ISAAC NEWTON

SIR ISAAC NEWTON
1795

A drawing for the famous coloured monotype executed in 1795, of which two examples are known, one in the Tate Gallery, the other in private possession in the United States. In the pencil drawing the figure of Newton with his scroll and compasses faces to the left, the opposite way to that in the monotype, and there is less detail in the surroundings. The figure itself is very much the same. It has not usually been noticed that in the monotype Newton appears to be seated at the bottom of the sea, the water symbolising the materialism of Newton's philosophy. The evidences of this are the anemones attached to the rock, on which he is seated, and the sea-weeds waving in the current; but these do not appear in the drawing.

It is probable that the drawing once belonged to Frederick Tatham; it was afterwards in the collections of George Smith and Captain Fenwick-Owen. A companion drawing of Sir Christopher Wren is in existence and was in George Smith's collection in 1880, but it is now lost to sight.

7 $^7/_8$ × 10 IN.   SIR GEOFFREY KEYNES

9

THE VIRGIN MARY HUSHING THE

YOUNG BAPTIST

THE VIRGIN MARY HUSHING THE
YOUNG BAPTIST

A pencil drawing on tracing paper for the tempera painting now in private possession in the United States. The infant Christ is lying asleep on a couch, watched over by his Mother, who admonishes the young St John approaching from the right with a butterfly in his hand. The curtain over the couch is marked 'Red', which is its colour in the painting.

The drawing was in the John Linnell collection until 1918, when it was acquired by Mr Vernon Wethered.

10 $^5/_8$ × 15 IN.   SIR GEOFFREY KEYNES

10

CATHERINE BLAKE

CATHERINE BLAKE

A drawing of Mrs Blake in middle life, probably done about 1803, since it is drawn on the back of a proof of page 9 of Hayley's *Ballads*, 1802. She is seated looking down at her hands on her lap. Inscribed "Catherine" by Blake and "Mrs Blake Drawn by Blake" by Frederick Tatham.

From the collection of Mrs Alexander Gilchrist; it later belonged to Miss A. G. E. Carthew, who bequeathed it to the Tate Gallery in 1940.

10 × 8 IN.   TATE GALLERY, LONDON

Mrs Blake
drawn by Blake

II

PESTILENCE

PESTILENCE

ABOUT 1805

Sketch of a nude figure seen from behind with arms outstretched and striding forwards. Vague masses on either side may indicate other figures. Another quite different drawing interpreted as representing the same subject from the collection in the British Museum was reproduced in the first series of *Pencil Drawings*, 1927.

$5\,^1/_4 \times 7\,^1/_4$ IN.

ROSENWALD COLLECTION, NATIONAL GALLERY OF ART, WASHINGTON, D.C.

12

EVE TEMPTED BY THE SERPENT

EVE TEMPTED BY THE SERPENT

ABOUT 1807

An early study of Eve and the Serpent for the water colour painting included in both the series of designs for *Paradise Lost*, one of which is in the H. E. Huntington Library, California, the other in the Boston Museum of Fine Arts. Eve is standing in front of the Tree, and the Serpent, with his coils around her body, presents the forbidden fruit to her mouth. The composition is considerably modified in the finished designs.

From the Tatham, George Smith, and Aspland collections.

9 × 5 IN.   VICTORIA AND ALBERT MUSEUM, LONDON

13

ADAM AND EVE

ADAM AND EVE

ABOUT 1807

A tiny sketch of the central figures in the water colour painting of "Satan watches Adam and Eve" formerly in the Sidney Morse collection and now in the Fogg Art Museum, Harvard University, Cambridge, Mass. It is drawn on the back of a portion of a letter in an unknown hand, and is inscribed by Blake "Adam & Eve".

$2\,^1/_2 \times 1\,^3/_4$ IN.   SIR GEOFFREY KEYNES

A larger drawing of the same subject with an indication of Satan floating above the heads of Adam and Eve, as in the finished painting.

Given to the British Museum by John Defett Francis in 1874.

$5 \times 5\,^1/_2$ IN.   BRITISH MUSEUM

14

SATAN COMES TO THE GATES OF HELL

SATAN COMES TO THE GATES OF HELL

ABOUT 1807

A pencil drawing with some pen and water colour washes
added. The subject is a preliminary sketch for the second
design in the series of twelve water colour drawings illustrating *Paradise Lost*, now in the Henry E. Huntington Library,
California. Satan on the left, with shield and spear, faces
the crowned figure of Death with his dart. Between them
is a woman described by Milton as:

> *a formidable shape;*
> *The one seem'd Woman to the waste, and fair*
> *But ended foul in many a scaly fould*
> *Voluminous and vast, a Serpent arm'd*
> *With mortal sting: about her middle round*
> *A cry of Hell Hounds never ceasing bark'd*
> *With wide Cerberean mouths full loud, and rung*
> *A hideous Peal: yet, when they list, would creep,*
> *If aught disturb'd their noyse, into her woomb,*
> *And kennel there, yet still bark'd and howl'd*
> *Within unseen.*

From the collection of Frederick Tatham.

$9\,^4/_5 \times 7\,^7/_{10}$ IN.   MR. & MRS. JOHN W. GARRETT (U.S.A.)

15

THE ANGEL OF THE RESURRECTION

THE ANGEL OF THE RESURRECTION

ABOUT 1808

A pencil sketch with some sepia washes added. An angel with a trumpet descends through clouds to awaken the dead, who are starting from their graves. The theme was a favourite one with Blake and he used it with great effect on the titlepage of Blair's *Grave* and elsewhere, but this version was not carried further in any of his finished designs.

Given to the British Museum by John Defett Francis in 1874.

4 ³/₈ × 3 ³/₈ IN.   BRITISH MUSEUM

16

THE MEETING OF A FAMILY IN HEAVEN

THE MEETING OF A FAMILY IN HEAVEN

ABOUT 1808

A vigorous sketch of a father and child meeting the mother at the Gates of Heaven. Two angels with keys are standing on the left. This was no doubt a preliminary study for the design in plate III of the illustrations for Blair's *Grave*, though it is entirely different from the tame and unemotional composition engraved by Schiavonetti for the book published in 1808.

Given to the British Museum by John Defett Francis in 1874.

$8\,^7/_8 \times 11\,^5/_8$ IN.   BRITISH MUSEUM

THE SOUL HOVERING OVER
THE BODY

THE SOUL HOVERING OVER
THE BODY
ABOUT 1808

A study for the illustration in Blair's *Grave*, 1808, plate v, of "The Soul hovering over the Body reluctantly parting with Life", though the final composition is much altered. In the drawing the Body is that of a nude muscular young man lying on his left side. In the engraving the Body lies supine clad in a long robe, and the Soul, instead of hovering horizontally over it, floats away in a graceful curve.

Formerly in the possession of Frederick Tatham. Bequeathed to the Tate Gallery by Sir Hugh Walpole in 1941.

10 $\frac{1}{4}$ × 17 $\frac{1}{2}$ IN.   TATE GALLERY, LONDON

UNIDENTIFIED SUBJECT

UNIDENTIFIED SUBJECT

A rough pencil sketch of an unidentified subject. In the centre a youthful nude figure springs up with outstretched arms to grasp an object hanging from the bough of a tree. On the left a tall figure hides his face in his hand. Another sorrowing figure kneels on the right close to the trunk of the tree.

Given to the British Museum by John Defett Francis in 1874.

8 $^7/_8$ × 11 $^1/_8$ IN.   BRITISH MUSEUM

19

MIRTH

MIRTH

One of a series of slight sketches marked respectively by Blake "The Three Tabernacles", "The Church Yard", "Death", "Mirth", "Hope". It is not known what significance he attached to them.

From the Tatham and Graham Robertson collections.

6 × 4 IN.   SIR GEOFFREY KEYNES

20

ALLEGORICAL DESIGN WITH A
RIVER GOD

ALLEGORICAL DESIGN WITH A RIVER GOD

Sketch for a complicated allegorical design, which is not wholly comprehended. A bearded River God is seated by his culvert on the right and gazes benevolently at a woman poised with outstretched arms in the water. A spirit descends from the clouds to clasp her head, and a nude, demonic impersonation seated on the left raises his hands in fear. A small human body lies prone on the demon's thigh. The River God was used with alterations in Blake's fourth design for Gray's "Ode on a Distant Prospect of Eton College". A bathing school boy there replaces the symbolic woman. The descending spirit is reminiscent of the figure of St John the Divine in the well-known painting, "The River of Life", and in no. 96 of the Dante series.

7 ½ × 14 IN.

VICTORIA AND ALBERT MUSUEM, LONDON

21

THE BARD, FROM GRAY

THE BARD, FROM GRAY
1809

A large sketch for the tempera painting dated 1809 now in the Tate Gallery. The Bard with his harp stands on a rock, below which King Edward and Queen Eleanor crouch in a confused heap. The spirits of other bards slain by the King float in the air above. There is another version of the sketch, touched with pen and wash, on the other side of the sheet.

From the collection of Richard Johnson sold in 1912.

$24^3/_4 \times 17^3/_4$ IN.   PHILADELPHIA MUSEUM OF ART

22

THE BOWMAN

THE BOWMAN

A vigorous sketch of a Bowman, with the personification of Inspiration stretching over him. The subject seems to illustrate the lines beginning:

"Bring me my bow of burning gold"

in the Preface to Blake's illuminated book, *Milton*, 1804–1808, but the subject is not otherwise known among his compositions.

From the Graham Robertson collection. Earlier provenance unknown.

$7\,^1/_2 \times 8\,^1/_2$ IN.　　　　　SIR GEOFFREY KEYNES

23

NUDE MALE FIGURES

NUDE MALE FIGURES

A series of studies of male bodies in various attitudes. They cannot be identified as belonging to any particular composition.

$5\,^1/_4 \times 8\,^1/_2$ IN.

PHILIP H. AND A. S. W. ROSENBACH FOUNDATION,
PHILADELPHIA, PA.

24

LOS SUPPORTING THE SUN

LOS SUPPORTING THE SUN

A sketch of a youthful nude figure supporting the orb of the sun on his upraised arms. The subject has been called "Figure holding the moon over his head", but that the orb is the sun and not the moon is shewn by the flames streaming from its rim with lightning zig-zagging on either side. The figure probably, therefore, represents Los, the Spirit of Poetry. The orb of the earth is indicated at the bottom between his legs. The design was not used elsewhere as far as is known.

The provenance of the drawing is not recorded.

7 × 5 IN.

ROSENWALD COLLECTION, NATIONAL GALLERY OF ART, WASHINGTON, D.C.

25

LOS KNEELING

LOS KNEELING

A nude figure, perhaps representing Los, the Spirit of Poetry, kneeling with his thighs apart. He has flame-like hair and his hands raised above his head carry an arrow in the left and (apparently) a sickle in the right. There is a background of flames.

9 $^{13}/_{16}$ × 12 $^{1}/_{4}$ IN.   YALE UNIVERSITY ART GALLERY

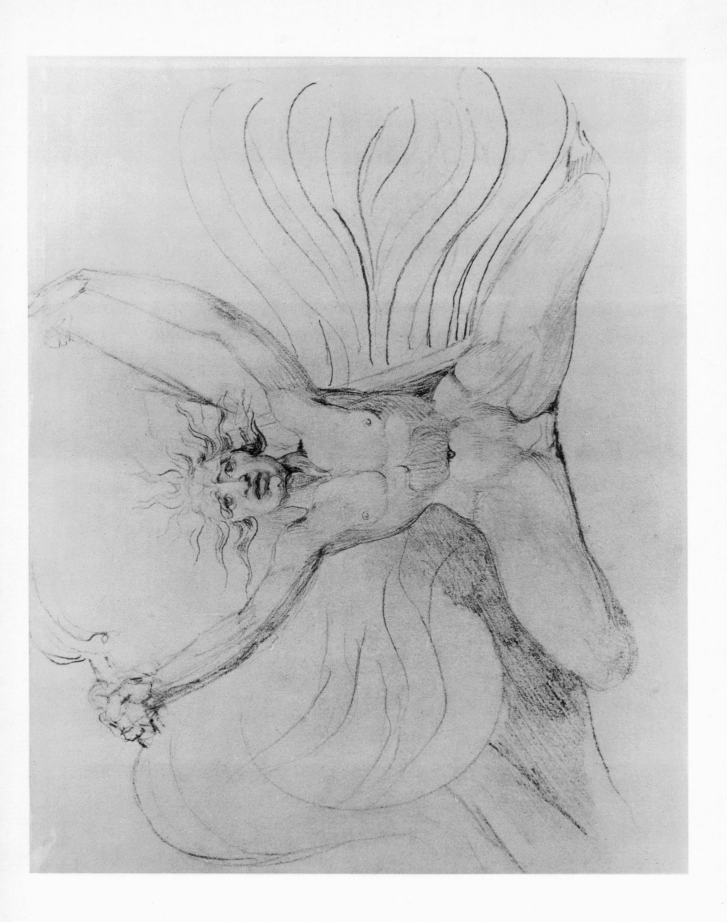

26

THE DESCENT OF PEACE

THE DESCENT OF PEACE
1809

A sketch for the first of six water colour designs illustrating Milton's ode "On the Morning of Christ's Nativity", of which two sets are extant, one in the Whitworth Institute, Manchester, the other in the Henry E. Huntington Library, San Marino, California. The Angel of Peace descends head downwards over the stable in which Mary is seen swooning into the arms of Joseph, who stands behind her. The infant Christ is springing from her body, and Elizabeth with the young St John kneels before her. Cattle are feeding from a manger in the background. Nature, as a nude woman, lies below in adoration.

The drawing resembles the design in the Huntington set more than that in the other, in which the Infant is folded in Mary's arms and Nature lies with her head to the left instead of to the right.

The sheet is inscribed below in Tatham's hand: "sketched by / William Blake / vouched / by Fredk Tatham".

$9\,^1/_2 \times 7\,^1/_4$ IN.

ROSENWALD COLLECTION, NATIONAL GALLERY OF ART, WASHINGTON, D.C.

Sketched by
William Blake
touched
by Mrs Tatham

27

A VISION OF THE LAST JUDGMENT

A VISION OF THE LAST JUDGMENT
1810

A large pencil drawing, worked over with indian ink and some touches of water colour wash. Christ sits in judgment in the upper part of this very elaborate composition containing hundreds of figures. The large tempera painting of The Last Judgment described by Blake in his long prose piece: "For the Year 1810 Additions to Blake's Catalogue of Pictures &c"*, has been lost, but there are several other versions, two in water colour and three in pencil. The drawings done only in pencil are less suitable for reproduction than the one here chosen, with the lines strengthened with indian ink. Blake's description of the lost painting is the best guide to the details of the drawing, though the two compositions are not exactly the same.

$17\,^7/_8 \times 15\,^5/_8$ IN.

ROSENWALD COLLECTION, NATIONAL GALLERY OF ART,

WASHINGTON, D.C.

* *Poetry and Prose*, ed. Keynes, 1939, p. 637.

28

TIME'S TRIPLE BOW

TIME'S TRIPLE BOW

FROM JERUSALEM

A scribbled, but powerful, sketch of Time with a triple bow riding a swift horse. The finished design appears at the top of plate 35 of *Jerusalem* (plate 39 in the Stirling copy). Of this Wicksteed writes: "The figure on the horse symbolises in ferocious form the ticking of the clock of fate, shooting shaft after shaft of anguish and fear into Man's mundane lot."* In the *Jerusalem* design Time is furnished with bat-wings, the symbol of the Arch-fiend.

The provenance of the drawing is unknown.

$12\,^{1}/_{2} \times 9\,^{1}/_{2}$ IN.

ROSENWALD COLLECTION, NATIONAL GALLERY OF ART, WASHINGTON, D.C.

* *William Blake's Jerusalem* (Commentary by Joseph Wicksteed), The William Blake Trust, (1952). p. 169.

29

ALBION AND THE LETTER THAT KILLETH

ALBION AND THE LETTER THAT KILLETH

FROM JERUSALEM

A careful drawing for the design occupying the lower half of plate 41 of *Jerusalem* (as arranged in the Stirling copy). The giant figure of Albion is seated on a rock with his face buried in the book of the Mosaic Law, which is spread open on his knees. In *Jerusalem* a scroll is added on Albion's right, carrying an inscription in reversed writing; a small figure is seated at the bottom of the scroll on the part still rolled up and gazes up at him.

$6^1/_2 \times 9^1/_4$ IN.

ROSENWALD COLLECTION, NATIONAL GALLERY OF ART, WASHINGTON, D.C.

30

LAOCOÖN

LAOCOÖN

ABOUT 1815

A drawing made by Blake about 1815 from a cast for an engraving in Rees's *Encyclopaedia*, published in 1820. Frederick Tatham has written below the drawing: "This drawing was made by Mr. Blake in the Royal Academy Somerset House for a small plate he made of the Laocoön for the Article in the Encyclopaedia. The article itself was on Sculpture being written by Mr. Flaxman. When Mr. B. was drawing this his old friend Fuseli came in & said 'Why Mr. Blake you a student you might teach us' in my possession from Mrs. Blake". About 1818 Blake made another engraving from this drawing, the large Laocoön plate, to which he added aphorisms on Art and Religion wherever he could find room. The figures were also given symbolical meanings, being designated *Jehovah & his two Sons Satan & Adam*, the serpents being marked *Good* and *Evil*. Blake also made an entirely different drawing, reproduced on the next page, giving his own version of the group.

The first drawing, after it was sold with Tatham's collection in 1862, belonged to Alfred Aspland, and was later in the Graham Robertson collection.

12 ⁵/₈ × 9 IN.   MR. HENRY J. CROCKER (U.S.A.)

This drawing was made by M.r Blake in the Royal
Academy Somerset House for a small plate he made of the
Laocoön for the Article in the Encyclopedia. the Article itself
on Sculpture being written by Flaxman. when M.r B up a draw
his his old friend Fuseli stood [illegible] [illegible]

31

LAOCOÖN — BLAKE'S VERSION:

LAOCOÖN—BLAKE'S VERSION

ABOUT 1815

The reproduction on the previous page shews Blake's drawing of the classic Laocoön group. He afterwards made
his own, entirely different, version of the group in the
pencil drawing reproduced opposite. Laocoön, that is, Jehovah, is struggling in the coils of the serpents, Good and
Evil, together with his sons, Satan and Adam, but the central figure is now clothed in a long robe. In *A Descriptive
Catalogue*, 1809, p. 59, Blake had written: "I understand
that my costume [in his picture of The Bramins] is incor-
rect, but in this I plead the authority of the ancients, who
often deviated from the Habits, to preserve the Manners, as
in the instance of Laocoön, who, though a priest, is represented naked." In his own representation of the group he
has therefore corrected this irregularity. Parts of the drawing, notably the left foot, have been carefully worked up
with the pen, and a few touches of water colour wash have
been added, the face of the central figure being tinged with
pink.

The drawing was sold with Tatham's collection in 1862;
it belonged later to George Smith and to Mrs. Lucy Graham Smith.

21 × 17 $^{1}/_{4}$ IN.   SIR GEOFFREY KEYNES

32

WAT TYLER'S DAUGHTER

WAT TYLER'S DAUGHTER
1819

A Visionary Head of Wat Tyler's daughter, and so marked by John Linnell at the top right-hand corner. Wat, or Walter, a tyler of Maidstone, was one of the leaders of the rebellion of 1381 against King Richard II. He is usually credited with having started the rising by killing a tax collector who had insulted his daughter, though it was really (according to the Stowe MS—*vide* D.N.B.) a John Tyler of Dartford who committed this deed. The girl is represented by Blake as a foolish-looking person with a wide face. The drawing is on paper watermarked *C Brenchley 1804*, but it was no doubt done at the same time as another of "Wat Tyler... from his spectre as in the Act of Striking the Tax Gatherer on the head Drawn Octr 30 1819 I h A.M."

In the Linnell collection until 1918.

$9^{1}/_{2} \times 7^{1}/_{4}$ IN.

ROSENWALD COLLECTION, NATIONAL GALLERY OF ART, WASHINGTON, D.C.

33

THE SPIRIT OF VOLTAIRE

THE SPIRIT OF VOLTAIRE
ABOUT 1820

The head of a man, which might be thought to have some resemblance to Blake himself. The dilated nostrils and the hair curling up from the forehead, as in the portrait of Blake by Phillips, suggest the likeness; but the drawing is inscribed below, in an unknown hand, "The Spirit of Voltaire". There is little resemblance to the usual images of Voltaire.

The provenance of the drawing is unknown.

9 × 6 IN.   DR. JOHN LIPSCOMB

The spirit of Voltaire By Blake

34

GOD CREATING THE UNIVERSE

GOD CREATING THE UNIVERSE
ABOUT 1788*

A pencil drawing inked over in two inks. Inscribed in pencil, but not in Blake's hand: "When he prepared the heavens, I was there, when he set a compass upon the face of the depth. Proverbs Chap 8. v. 27".

This drawing is quite different from the well-known design with the same title etched and coloured by Blake as the frontispiece to *Europe*, 1794, in which the Creator is on one knee facing the spectator and reaching down into the void with his compass. In the drawing reproduced here a figure in a long gown crouches on the ground on both knees and is seen from the side, the compasses being sketched in two positions. It is probably the earlier of the two designs, since it appears to be a study for the small plate in *There is No Natural Religion*, second series, done about 1788. Here the subject is etched below the text: *Application. He who sees the Infinite in all things sees God. He who sees the Ratio only sees himself only.*** The crouching figure is beneath the over-arching branches of a tree, and his compass is reflected as a triangle on the ground, suggesting that the design really represents the rational man gazing at the ground and seeing himself only.

The provenance of the drawing is unknown before 1912, when it was first sold at auction.

9 × 12 ½ IN.   MRS RUTH LOWINSKY

*This drawing is here out of its proper order, the decision to include it having been made too late to place it early in the sequence.
**The only known impression of this plate is in my collection.

"When he prepared the Heavens
I was there; when he set a compass
upon the face of the depth."
Proverbs Chap 8 v 2

35

URIAH AND BATHSHEBA

URIAH AND BATHSHEBA

c. 1820

The two visionary heads are drawn side by side in profile to the left. The woman, on the right, is marked "Bathsheba"; the man is inscribed "Uriah the Husband of Bathsheba".

From the John Linnell collection.

$8\,^1/_4 \times 12\,^7/_8$ IN.

Bathsheba

Sarah the Husband
of Bathsheba

7

JOSEPH AND MARY AND THE ROOM
THEY WERE SEEN IN

JOSEPH AND MARY AND THE ROOM THEY WERE SEEN IN

ABOUT 1820

A careful drawing of the youthful pair, their heads inclining towards one another, Mary with her hands crossed on her breast. Between them is a small drawing of "the room they were seen in", presumably in Blake's vision. The figures are in the same attitudes as in the larger drawings, but the boy is being led away by a bearded man, perhaps his father. In the background is a bed with a canopy. The title is inscribed on the back of the sheet. This drawing belongs to the series of "Visionary Heads" done for Linnell and Varley.

From the John Linnell collection.

$7\,^7/_8 \times 12\,^3/_8$ IN.

HENRY E. HUNTINGTON LIBRARY AND ART GALLERY,
SAN MARINO, CALIFORNIA

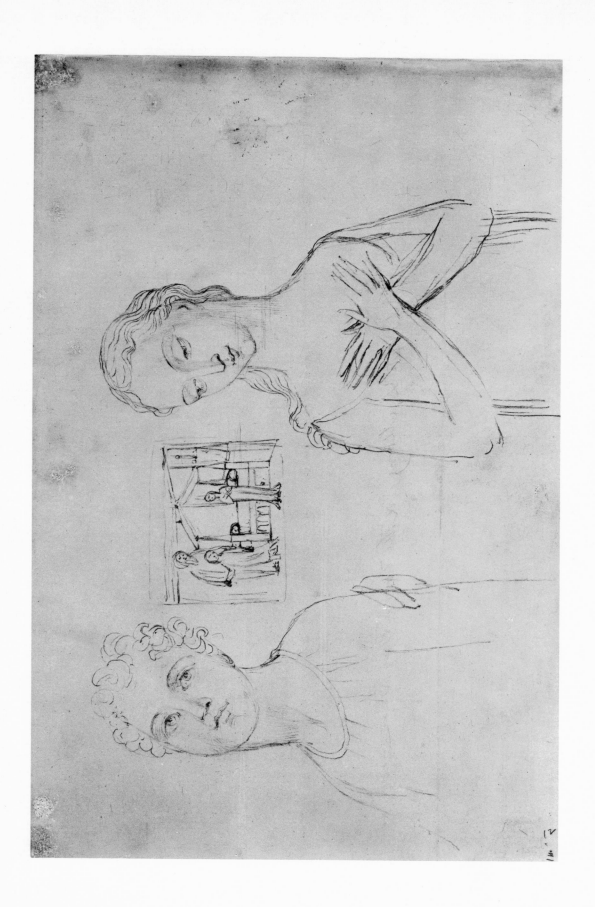

37

FRIAR BACON AND THE POET GRAY

FRIAR BACON AND THE POET GRAY

ABOUT 1820

On the right is a drawing of a "visionary head" of Roger Bacon, the thirteenth century Franciscan philosopher, with the name written below. Near the left margin is an outline of Thomas Gray's face in profile, marked "Gray the Poet". The resemblance to Gray is unmistakable, if slightly caricatured; Blake had perhaps seen the drawing of the poet in profile by James Basire, now in the National Portrait Gallery, after the posthumous drawing by the Rev. William Mason.

From the John Linnell collection.

$7\,^3/_4 \times 6\,^3/_8$ IN. PEMBROKE COLLEGE, CAMBRIDGE

Friar Bacon

38

OLD PARR WHEN YOUNG

OLD PARR WHEN YOUNG

1820

A careful drawing of a nude, thickset, youngish man with long hair onto his shoulders. The hands and left foot are unfinished. Written below on the left is: "Old Parr when young viz 40", and, on the other side, "Aug 1820—W Blake fect". Thomas Parr was an old countryman, who died in 1653 at the reputed age of 153. He had been brought up to London to be shewn to the King and was given food of unaccustomed richness, which proved fatal. A *postmortem* was performed by Dr. William Harvey, who found all his organs to be quite healthy. It may be noted that "Old Parr" resembles in its essentials "The Symbolic Figure of the Course of Human History described by Virgil", no. 28 in the series of designs for Dante's *Divine Comedy*. It has been suggested that Blake derived his conception of this figure from "some antique statue of Helios", but it seems more probable that he had to seek no further than his own imaginary idea of Old Parr as recorded for Varley in 1820.

From the John Linnell collection.

11 3/4 × 7 1/4 IN.

HENRY E. HUNTINGTON LIBRARY AND ART GALLERY, SAN MARINO, CALIFORNIA

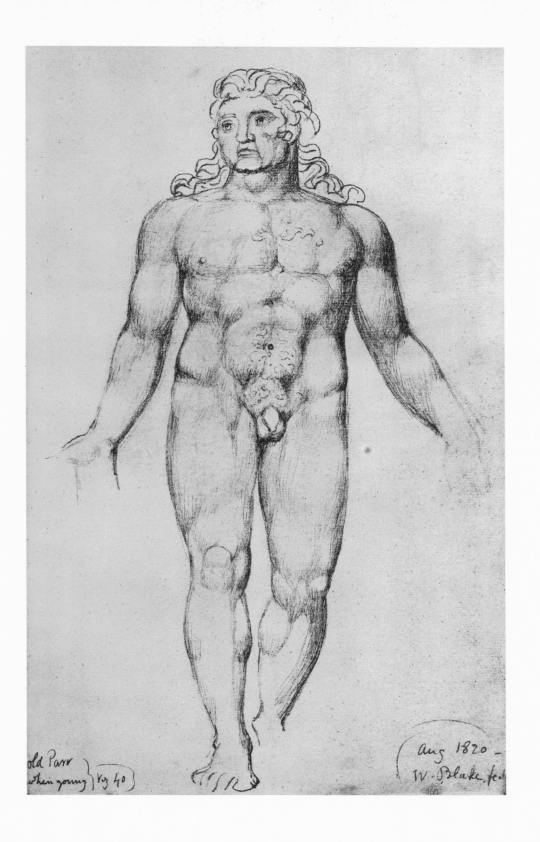

Old Parr
when young
Vg 40

aug 1820 -
W. Blake fc

39

ISAIAH FORETELLING THE

CRUCIFIXION

ISAIAH FORETELLING THE CRUCIFIXION

ABOUT 1821

One of two sketches for the drawing on a woodblock now in the British Museum, Department of Prints and Drawings. The finished drawing, which was never actually cut on the wood, shews, above the Prophet, "the Destruction of Jerusalem", but Blake's intention was different at first, the scene in the pencil sketch shewing the Crucifixion and Ascension with the Holy Spirit as a Dove in the centre. Below the drawing is an inscription by Samuel Palmer: "The first Lines on the preservation of which Mr. Blake used so often to insist are on the other side". There is a repetition of the drawing on the other side of the sheet, but the one reproduced here is more like the finished drawing and is likely to have been done second.

From the collection of Samuel Palmer.

$4^{3}/_{4} \times 3$ IN.   BRITISH MUSEUM

The "First Lines" on the preservation of which Mr. Blake used so often to insist are on the other side.

40

THE CIRCLE OF THE LIFE OF MAN

THE CIRCLE OF THE LIFE OF MAN
1821

A large drawing formerly known as "The River of Oblivion", but now related to the picture interpreted as "The Circle of the Life of Man", painted in 1821 and discovered at Arlington Court, near Barnstaple, Devon. The drawing omits many important features seen in the finished picture. It shews the central group of the Ideal Man, or Adam Cadmon, about to plunge into the Sea of Time and Space (not seen here), with his Emanation, Vala, standing behind him. Below is the River of Death with floating figures, and on the right are women weaving the tapestry of Fate, with one carrying a bucket of water from the river. In the centre is a young girl seated at the foot of a tree, carrying the skein of the Thread of Life on her raised hands. For a fuller interpretation of this highly symbolical composition reference can be made to my article in the volume, *Studies in Art and Literature for Belle da Costa Greene*, Princeton, 1954.

The drawing belonged formerly to John Flaxman and later to his sister-in-law, Maria Denman.

$15\,^1/_2 \times 18\,^1/_2$ IN. THE PIERPONT MORGAN LIBRARY, NEW YORK

41

SATAN

SATAN

ABOUT 1823

A rough sketch of Satan seen from behind carrying a sword; it resembles the small figure engraved at the top of plate 4 of the *Illustrations of the book of Job*, 1825, inscribed: "Going to & fro in the Earth & walking up & down in it". In the engraving the figure is reversed and has huge spiked wings added. The drawing is inscribed at the bottom: "Drawn by William Blake vouched by Fredk. Tatham".

From the Tatham and Graham Robertson collections.

$8\frac{1}{2} \times 5$ IN.   SIR GEOFFREY KEYNES

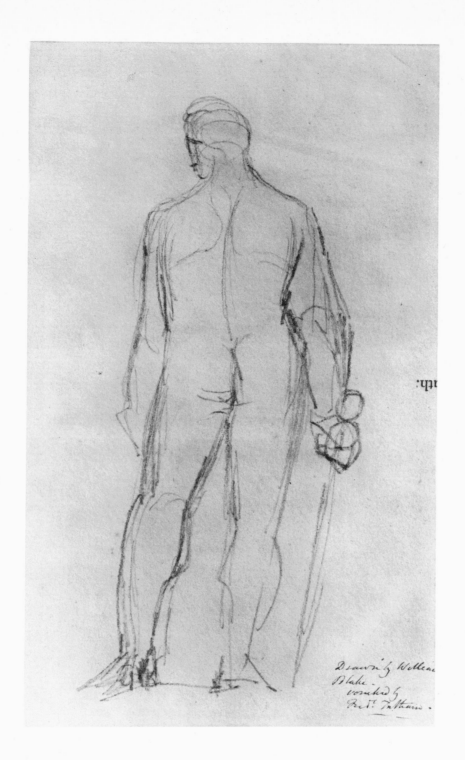

Drawn by William
Blake.
vouched by
Fred[?] Tatham.

42

JOB AND HIS DAUGHTERS

JOB AND HIS DAUGHTERS

ABOUT 1824

A preliminary sketch for the design in plate 20 of the *Illustrations of the Book of Job*, 1825. There are several versions in water colour or pencil besides the engraving, but usually the group is shewn inside a room with frescoes on the wall behind. In this sketch the scene is set without, the sun being indicated over Job's head and with suggestions of sheep on either side.

From the collection of Mrs. Alexander Gilchrist.

8 1/2 × 10 IN.

ROSENWALD COLLECTION, NATIONAL GALLERY OF ART, WASHINGTON, D.C.

43

EVERY MAN ALSO GAVE HIM A
PIECE OF MONEY

EVERY MAN ALSO GAVE HIM A
PIECE OF MONEY

ABOUT 1824

A preliminary sketch, slightly tinted, for the subject of plate 19 of the *Illustrations of the Book of Job*, 1825. The design was, however, entirely changed for the engraving. In the sketch Job and his wife are seated in the centre receiving presents from groups of people on either side with an almost selfrighteous air. Jehovah and his angels float over their heads. In the engraving Job and his wife are seated on the right in attitudes of deep humility, while four friends are bringing gifts towards them. The heavenly group is omitted. In the British Museum, Department of Prints and Drawings, there is a second tinted sketch of the same design as is reproduced here, shewing only minor changes, though less carefully drawn.

From the Tatham, Weston, and Graham Robertson collections.

$8\,^{15}/_{16} \times 6\,^{15}/_{16}$ IN.   KERRISON PRESTON ESQ

44

JOHN LINNELL

JOHN LINNELL
1825

This lightly drawn portrait of Blake's friend and
benefactor was done in 1825 when Linnell was aged
33. Blake had known him for eight years and was
just completing the engraved *Illustrations of the
Book of Job* done at Linnell's instigation and with
his financial help. The drawing shews a youngish
man, though somewhat plumper in the face than the
image drawn by Linnell himself "as a young man",
reproduced in Story's *Life of Linnell*, 1892, vol. I,
frontispiece. The sheet is inscribed below, probably
by Linnell: "at Hampstead / Drawn by Mr. Blake /
from the life 1825. / intended as The Portrait of J.
Linnell". The drawing was in the Linnell collection
until 1918.

9 × 6 ³/₄ IN.

ROSENWALD COLLECTION, NATIONAL GALLERY OF
ART, WASHINGTON, D.C.

at Hampstead
Drawn by Mr Blake
from the life 1825
intended as the Portrait
of J. Linnell

ILLUSTRATIONS OF THE BOOK OF ENOCH

An English translation of the Ethiopic *Book of Enoch* was published at Oxford in 1821 and may have been read by Blake at any time in the last six years of his life. It has been noted that parts of this book bear some likeness to Dante's *Divine Comedy*, which engrossed Blake's mind during the last years of his life, and it is therefore probable that it was during this period that he made the five pencil drawings, each of which is endorsed "Book of Enoch". The drawings are all preliminary studies, but they are not known to have been developed any further. The meaning of the drawings was first elucidated by their former owner, Allan R. Brown, of New Rochester, N.Y., in an article in the *Burlington Magazine*, LXXVII, September, 1940.

The first three drawings (here numbers 45, 46, 47) illustrate passages in the *Book of Enoch* describing the Fall of the Angels and their subsequent degeneration:

"And it came to pass in the days when the children of men had multiplied that there were born unto them beautiful and comely daughters. And the angels, the children of heaven, saw and lusted after them, and said to one another, 'Come, let us choose wives for ourselves from among the daughters of man and beget us children'. And they were in all two hundred, who descended and took unto themselves wives, and each chose for himself one; and they began to go in unto them and to defile themselves with them, and they taught them charms and enchantments and the cutting of roots, and made them acquainted with plants, and revealed to them all kinds of sin.

And they became pregnant and bare great giants, whose height was three thousand ells. And these consumed all the acquisitions of men. And when men could no longer sustain them, the giants turned against them and devoured mankind.

And there arose much godlessness, and they committed fornication and were led astray and became corrupt in all their ways. And the whole earth was filled with blood and unrighteousness. And the women also of the angels who went astray became sirens."

The fourth and fifth design (48 and 49) represent the Godhead and the Messiah. The five drawings were in the John Linnell collection, and were acquired by Allan R. Brown. ABOUT 21 × 14 1/2 IN.

THE BOOK OF ENOCH

(a)

Two angels in the form of stars with phallic attributes descend towards one of the beautiful daughters of men.

46

THE BOOK OF ENOCH

(b)

THE BOOK OF ENOCH

(b)

An angel rushes down to whisper the secrets of sin in the ear of a daughter of man. On either side are giant offspring, with flowers and plants. Flames stream upwards from the giant on the left.

47

THE BOOK OF ENOCH

(c)

THE BOOK OF ENOCH

(c)

The woman, now become a siren, rises exultingly to the left from the prostrate body of a man lying at the foot of a tree. Another, innocent, woman stands horrified at the other side of the tree.

48

THE BOOK OF ENOCH

(d)

THE BOOK OF ENOCH
(d)

Enoch with his guiding angel stands before the Great Glory on the steps of his throne. On either side are the heads of angels whose great wings arch over the throne.

49

THE BOOK OF ENOCH

(e)

THE BOOK OF ENOCH

(e)

The Son of Man, or Messiah, surrounded by four
attendant spirits. The arms of the two at the sides
form an arch over his head. The two lower ones are
beneath his feet.

50

UNIDENTIFIED SUBJECT

UNIDENTIFIED SUBJECT

ABOUT 1826

Sketch in Blake's later manner for a subject perhaps related to the five designs for *The Book of Enoch*. An "angel" with flames radiating from his head approaches another nude figure seen from behind. The angel's arms are outstretched and he holds a knife in his right hand. A rope, or tassel, hangs from the elbow of each arm. An indefinite figure is crouched on the ground between the other two. On either side is a mass of stone.

At the lower right hand corner Blake has written a word, perhaps "Men", in ink, but it is smudged and hard to decipher.

Given to the British Museum by John Defett Francis in 1874.

7 ³/₄ × 6 ¹/₄ IN.   BRITISH MUSEUM

51

DESIGN PERHAPS FOR DANTE'S

DIVINE COMEDY

DESIGN PERHAPS FOR DANTE'S
DIVINE COMEDY

ABOUT 1826

A sketchy drawing of uncertain meaning. It has been taken to be a study for the "Circle of the Lustful", no. 10 of the Dante series, but this is very doubtful. The identification might be based on the clockwise motion of the floating figures, as in the "Circle of the Lustful", and by supposing that the figures embracing on the right represent Paolo and Francesca. The indefinite figures on the extreme right might be Virgil and Dante.

The provenance is unknown.

$9 \times 5\frac{1}{4}$ IN.

52

THE VESTIBULE OF HELL AND THE

SOULS MUSTERING TO CROSS

THE ACHERON

THE VESTIBULE OF HELL AND
THE SOULS MUSTERING TO
CROSS THE ACHERON

DANTE *Inferno* CANTO III

ABOUT 1826

A preliminary sketch for no. 5 of the Dante series. The finished water-colour, now in the National Gallery of Victoria, Melbourne, is very different in its proportions and is overcrowded, but the essentials are similar. Dante and Virgil stand on a rocky ledge on the right. In the centre are congregated the souls of the damned, with one carrying a flag on a pole at their head. Part of Charon's boat is just visible on the extreme left. There is a vague background of rocky hills.

Given to the British Museum by John Defett Francis in 1874.

$9\,^1/_4 \times 7\,^7/_8$ IN.   BRITISH MUSEUM

53

THE USURERS

THE USURERS

DANTE'S *Inferno,* CANTO XVII

ABOUT 1826

A sketch for no. 30 of the Dante series, not taken any further. Dante looks at the four usurers seated on the ground with large purses carrying escutcheons round their necks, by which they may be identified. A few lines have been inked, and there is a touch of red water colour paint on the mouth of the usurer nearest Dante.

From the John Linnell collection.

$9^{1}/_{2} \times 13^{1}/_{2}$ IN.

FOGG MUSEUM OF ART, HARVARD UNIVERSITY,
CAMBRIDGE, MASS.

54

THE SIX-FOOTED SERPENT ATTACKING
BRUNELLESCHI

THE SIX-FOOTED SERPENT
ATTACKING BRUNELLESCHI

DANTE'S *Inferno*, CANTO XXV

ABOUT 1827

A pencil drawing for the water colour, no. 51, in the Dante series. The finished design follows the pencil drawing very closely. Blake also engraved this subject, introducing minor variations. Dante and Virgil are watching the three robbers, Brunelleschi, Sciancato, and Buoso Donati. The fourth robber, Cianfa Donati, already transformed into a monster, springs onto Brunelleschi, and they are together transformed into a serpent.

$9\,^{11}/_{16} \times 12\,^{7}/_{8}$ IN.

HENRY E. HUNTINGTON LIBRARY AND ART GALLERY, SAN MARINO, CALIFORNIA

55

BRUNELLESCHI HALF TRANSFORMED

INTO A SERPENT

BRUNELLESCHI HALF TRANSFORMED INTO A SERPENT

DANTE'S *Inferno*, CANTO XXV

ABOUT 1827

A preliminary study for the larger drawing of "Brunelleschi half transformed into a serpent" in the series of illustrations of Dante's *Divine Comedy*, no. 52.

Provenance unknown. Found by the present owner in Dublin.

$9^{1}/_{2} \times 7$ IN.   MICHAEL AYRTON ESQ

56

DESIGN PERHAPS FOR DANTE'S

DIVINE COMEDY

DESIGN PERHAPS FOR DANTE'S DIVINE COMEDY

A sketch for a design suggesting a subject from Dante, but it does not resemble any of those in the Dante series. The figure on the right turning away in pity from the tormented figure in the centre might be that of Dante, but if so Virgil is not shewn. The drawing is on a leaf of a book shewing only the catch-word "With".

The provenance is unknown.

$8\,^3/_4 \times 4\,^1/_2$ IN.

THE PIERPONT MORGAN LIBRARY, NEW YORK